The List

Tools to create the life of your dreams

Rebecca Fisk

To my mom
Lili Lampl
whose love and guidance gave me the courage to believe
in myself.

In Gratitude

I am grateful, first and foremost, to my family. I have been (and can be) a bit of a challenge to understand with my non-traditional ideas, but they have always loved me no matter what. Like my husband says, "It's not always easy, but it's always love."

I am also grateful to my friends. I am blessed to have lifetime friends who have remained constant regardless of the changes in our lives. I believe there is no greater treasure than the love and support of someone who accepts and appreciates you just the way you are, and I am blessed to have that many times over.

To my clients; thank you. Without you, there would have been no impetus to write this book, nor would there be an audience to read it. I am grateful to you beyond measure.

To the practitioners who have helped me stay grounded and healthy through the years; Dr. Betty Ciuchta, David Chan, Laura Tree, Arlene Pantalone and Karola Creel; deepest gratitude for helping me keep my feet on the planet.

Thank you to those who have crossed my path, even for a brief time: I believe we learn something from each encounter, whether it's a smile from a stranger reflecting love to us, or discord with a coworker challenging us to acknowledge our deepest fears; we have an opportunity to learn about ourselves in every moment. For that, I am grateful.

And to Mata Amritanandamayi (Ammachi); your selflessness is an inspiration and your unconditional love is healing the world. Thank you for offering yourself to all of us so we can learn to understand the true meaning of love and compassion. Om Namah Shivaya[1].

---

[1] Sanskrit: "I honor the divine within."

Preface

Let me preface this book by stipulating that I am not a therapist. The suggestions in this book are intended to help facilitate the movement of energy in your life to create a more positive experience.

I have used these tools in my own life, but have also sought professional counsel when I felt I needed help.

If you need help, please call a qualified, licensed therapist in your area.

I wish each and every one of you the experience of knowing God's Grace in your life. Through the cooperative process of list writing, I believe you will!

Prologue

Writing lists is something I started doing in the 1990's. Several years passed before I realized everything I had ever written with clear intention had come to fruition.

Some years later "The Secret" and "The Law of Attraction" received a lot of attention and many people started creating vision boards to create their dream life. I, too, started creating visual reminders of what I wanted to manifest in my life. But what happened surprised me; the reminders I kept in front of me didn't come to fruition and, for a while, I couldn't understand why.

What finally occurred to me was one very important concept; we don't create our lives, we co-create our lives. In other words, there are always other energies working to support our highest good. Call it God, the Universe, whatever you like, but we are never truly alone and we are always receiving assistance.

When we create a vision board and leave it in front of us, we are, in a sense, holding on to the vision and not allowing the Universe to work on the manifestation of our vision. We are actually holding on to it too tightly, and nothing can grow in a "death" grip!

Think: "Let it go so it can grow!"

It works!!!

What follows is a simple, succinct method for list writing that will help you manifest your dreams. The clear vision, action and intention are up to you; the Universe will handle the rest!

I was asked to write this book by some of my clients. I have recommended list writing to people for many years to help them get clarity on what they want and to help bring that energy into their lives.

I have done list writing myself for years, so I know it works and does so in every area of life. Relationships, work, home - you name it, it works! I even found a list of items I had written about a car six months after I purchased the car. Every detail was there, including the color and the seat warmers, even though I didn't specify the brand of car.

I realize you may be thinking writing lists to get what you want sounds greedy and shallow. But it isn't really and here's why: we are here to learn and grow. God doesn't care if you drive a Maserati or a Ford; you can learn lessons in either car, and learning lessons is what we're here for. Hopefully, no matter what you choose to drive, you will learn to be a safe, responsible driver.

When it comes to setting intentions, it is very important to focus on the "what" not the "how". The "how" is up to the Universe, the "what" is up to you.

My husband told me a story about when he was 4 years old and his mom had taken him to a diner. When the waitress asked him what he wanted to order he said, "Oh, just whatever you want to bring me."

Of course, that is very cute, but most of us do not want to receive whatever is being randomly dished out!!!!

Another thing to consider is to add "For the Highest Good of all" at the end of all of your prayers. The reason I suggest this is important: ultimately this intention saves some heartache and hard lessons for people. The way it works is this:

Let's suppose Joe would like to be an airline pilot. Ultimately, Joe has always dreamed of being able to fly a Gulfstream jet anywhere in the world. So he goes to flight school and logs the many hours, takes the numerous tests, and finally, he has his pilot's license. In order to fly a Gulfstream, Joe has to receive some additional training and take some more tests, but it is worth it. As it turns out, he also qualifies to be a commercial pilot due to all the experience he has.

Now that Joe has what he needs, he is ready to go out and fly a Gulfstream jet. So he starts applying for jobs at private companies who have their own Gulfstream jets, but no one is hiring. One of his friends tells him about job openings at a commercial airline, but he declines, focusing only on flying Gulfstream jets.

After a few more weeks with no job, Joe is starting to become discouraged. He sees an ad in the local paper that another commercial airline is hiring pilots, but it's not a company with Gulfstream jets, so he pays no attention.

Two more weeks pass. Joe runs into a friend he knew in college and the friend tells Joe he is an airline pilot. Joe tells him he has recently acquired his pilot's license and he mentions that he wants to fly Gulfstream jets. The friend chuckles and says, "Everyone wants to fly Gulfstream jets!"

Before he leaves, the two exchange phone numbers and the friend mentions his airline is hiring pilots and has a preference for people who have just graduated from flight school. Joe tells him he is running out of savings and needs a job, but says he would prefer to hold out for a job flying Gulfstream jets.

A few days later, Joe is talking with a friend who asks how the job search is going. He tells her he is becoming frustrated because it seems there is no job for him. She smiles and tells him she understands exactly how he feels. She remembers Joe had previously mentioned to her all of the opportunities for commercial airline pilots, so she says, "Could it be the Universe is trying to give you an opportunity that is for the Highest Good and you aren't paying attention?"

Joe thinks about this for a minute and asks her what she means. She asks him if it ever occurred to him to check the corporate information of the airlines that were hiring. Some commercial airlines have separate divisions that involve smaller corporate accounts but require their pilots to first gain experience with the larger jetliners. Joe tells her he had never considered that possibility.

The next day, Joe looks for the newspaper ad to locate the name of a commercial airline that is hiring. He finds the name, does some research and finds out his friend was correct; the airline does, indeed, have smaller corporate accounts that include flying executives on Gulfstream jets.

He also calls the friend from college to get more information about that airline and finds out they, too, have smaller corporate accounts.

So Joe calls the two airlines, goes through the interview process and two months later is working as a pilot at a commercial airline.

He flies all over the world, but he still isn't flying Gulfstream jets. He has mentioned to the other pilots his interest in flying Gulfstream jets and three years later, one of the other pilots mentions an opening in the corporate division.

Joe interviews for the position and gets the job. Now he has the job of his dreams, even though the journey to get there wasn't what he thought it would be.

Are you ready? Let's get started.

Step One: Stream of Consciousness Writing

Get some paper and a pen and decide which topic you would like to work on. Is your greatest desire or need a new job, relationship or are you interested in a new home? It can be whatever you want.

Set the timer for 10 or 20 minutes. The length of time doesn't really matter, it should be a comfortable amount of time for YOU.

Start writing anything and everything that comes to mind on the topic. Do not edit right now; just write whatever pops into your head. Keep going until the timer goes off.

When the timer sounds, read over your list. If anything is listed as a negative statement, turn it into a positive statement.

For example, if you are working on a "perfect relationship" list and you've written "I want someone who doesn't smoke", change the statement to "I want a non-smoker". The Universe doesn't acknowledge whether or not there is a "do" or "don't" in front of the word; it just takes in the energy of the word.

After you have changed negative statements to positive statements, decide if there is anything you'd like to add or delete from the list. Once you feel satisfied that your list is complete, put it away. And I do mean put it AWAY - in a drawer or someplace where you will not see it every day.

In two to three weeks, get the list out again. Read it and decide if you would like to add anything else to the list. Be VERY specific!

I tell a joke about the fact that I found my relationship list two months after I started dating my husband. I remember thinking to myself "He's everything on my list. Now what do I do?" Well, now that I have been married to him for 10 years, there are a few things I would have added to that list! Such as, "a partner who doesn't work such long hours."

Below is another reason I advise people to be very specific and detailed about their desires:

I remember running into an acquaintance in January a few years ago. She asked me if I had made any New Year's resolutions. I told her I hadn't and she proceeded to tell me she had.

She told me her resolution was that she was going to start dating. She hadn't had a date in seven years and she was tired of being alone, so she was going to start dating. Well, her resolve and clear intention worked. Within two weeks she started meeting men everywhere; at the gas station, at the grocery store; it seemed like every time she turned a corner she was meeting another man.

The problem was this; one was married; another didn't

have a job; another drank a lot. She was becoming disillusioned very quickly.

I said. "That's because you weren't specific enough. You told the Universe "I want to date" and the Universe said "Okay, here are some men." But since you only had the intention of dating without clear qualities about the people you wanted to date, the Universe sent any and all men in your direction."

When you write a clear list, the Universe acknowledges it by limiting the possibilities to those who match the energy of what you have written. So it deletes the married men because you write that you want someone who is available to you in every way. It deletes the unemployed men because you write that you want a partner who has a great job, loves his work and is well-paid. It deletes the men who drink too much because you write that you want a partner who is sober and willing to stay present in all situations.

Include any attributes you want your perfect partner to have. Anything is okay - **REALLY! You are worth it!**

Step Two: Be willing to say "No" to what you don't want in order to have the opportunity to say "Yes" to what you do want.

What does that mean?

Here's an example; you have written your relationship list and forgotten about it. You meet a great looking, fun-loving, wonderful man. He is between jobs right now, but has some money in the bank and is certain he will have a job again in no time. He seems like the perfect guy, except he doesn't have a job and that was definitely on the list. What do you do?

I know it seems callous to dismiss someone as wonderful as this guy just because he doesn't have a job, but trust me, it is for the best. There are many reasons to not date a man who doesn't have a job, not the least of which is that his self-esteem will end up in the toilet before too long, but that is another book by another author (Dr. John Gray would be the expert on this!)

The reason you don't date someone who doesn't have a job if the job is on your list is because you didn't "order" him. WHAT?

When you go to a restaurant and the waitress takes your order, you assume your order will be made and delivered. You don't wonder if she got your order right or whether or not the cook will prepare the correct entrée, you just know the right thing is being prepared and will be brought to the table.

And, if the wrong dinner is brought to the table, you tell the waitress you didn't order it and she will bring the correct entrée!

I love to use another example; Filet Mignon. If you order Filet Mignon and the waitress brings you a hamburger, you have several choices; tell her to keep the hamburger and you will wait for the Filet Mignon; tell her you ordered the Filet Mignon, but keep the hamburger and eat it; don't tell her she made a mistake and eat the hamburger all the while wishing you'd told her because you really wanted the Filet Mignon!

In the first case, you get what you want. You say "No, thank you" to the hamburger and have a very satisfying, delectable Filet Mignon.

In the second case, you eat the hamburger, but are too full to eat the Filet Mignon when it comes to the table.

And in the third case, you eat the hamburger, don't get the Filet Mignon and you end up feeling resentment. You probably won't go back to that restaurant again and you may even tell people about the "lousy" experience you had. So, in the end, you're upset and the restaurant is getting a reputation for bad service, all because you didn't speak up.

It is always best to ask for what you want and to wait to

receive it!

Of course, I have had clients say "But what if this is supposed to be THE GUY and no one better will come along?"

Well, the Universe doesn't go backwards, it only moves forward. That means that each time you are willing to say no to what you don't want, another better and more appropriate match will show up. That doesn't mean you won't be given more opportunities to say "No, thank you," but I guarantee you that if something doesn't work out, there is another, better match for you on the way.

You may be wondering why our lists don't manifest instantly. Well, the Universe doesn't work in time/space like we do here on Earth, but it does work in perfect rhythm and timing for our highest good. In other words, if you have written a list, the Universe will bring that person to you when you and he or she are both ready.

Synchronicity is also at work here and there has to be some trust that the Universe knows what it's doing. It would be devastating to meet that perfect guy when he is still married to someone else!

Step Three: Be in love with yourself and your life

I remember when I started dating my husband. At the time, I thought to myself, "I love my life. Do I really want to complicate it with a relationship?"

Obviously, I did "complicate" it with a relationship. But, at the time, I was happy with my life and my happiness didn't depend on, someone else!

Happy people are attractive. People love to be around positive energy, so if you are radiating happiness and positive energy, you will naturally draw more people to you.

The more people you draw to you, the more opportunity you have to pick and choose those you want to be close to.

If you are not in love with your life, you may be asking "How do I fall in love with my life?"

The answer is very simple, really; start doing things that bring you joy and make you feel loved. For me, taking care of myself helped me feel more grounded and connected to God and the Universe.

Here are some suggestions:

1) walking at the beach
2) camping

3) hiking
4) baths with Epson salts, oils and candles
5) pedicures
6) massages
7) spending time with a loved and trusted partner
8) exercise
9) yoga
10) walking barefoot on the grass
11) eating very slowly, really tasting the food
12) burning incense or aromatherapy candles
13) listening to favorite music
14) dancing
15) spending quality time with trusted friends
16) reading a good book
17) listening to inspirational tapes
18) browsing at an art gallery or museum
19) finger-painting
20) molding something out of clay or using a pottery wheel
21) journaling
22) watching a comedy show or something that makes you laugh
23) visiting a beautiful garden and smelling the flowers
24) sitting in the sun
25) feeling the water as it hits your skin in the shower
26) swimming
27) baking or cooking
28) playing with your dog or cat
29) smiling!
30) calling a friend you love to talk to
31) volunteering

32) napping

These suggestions cost little or nothing. They are activities just for you, no one else. If you are going along with a friend to an exercise class because she doesn't want to go alone, you aren't doing it for yourself. Tell her "no, thank you" and do something for your own soul!

It may take a little practice to get into the habit of including one or more of these "soul treats" every day, but I guarantee you will start enjoying your life more if you do!

If you find you are having a difficult time feeling joy in your life, you may want to do some journaling to get in touch with your inner self. Sometimes we have unexpressed anger or sadness that is blocking our ability to experience real joy.

So many of us have had experiences that have caused us to become really hurt or angry, yet we haven't been taught how to release those emotions in a healthy way. I often suggest letter writing to clients to help them release these unexpressed emotions and I strongly suggest this be done at a time when you will be alone.

Step Four: Letter Writing

Start by getting some paper and pen or pencil and sit in a comfortable place. Think about someone who has caused significant distress in your life and write a letter to that person. Tell him or her everything you have ever wanted to say; bad or good, mean or loving; it doesn't matter. The purpose is to allow a safe channel for all of the emotions to come out of your body.

When you feel a sense of completion, i.e. peaceful and (probably) tired, burn the letter. If you don't have a fireplace, you can also shift the energy by tearing the letter into small pieces. As you burn or tear up the paper, offer a prayer for the emotions released to be transmuted into Light and Love for the Highest Good of All.

Some people have a hard time letting go of anger, frustration or sadness because they don't want to "pollute" the planet with bad energy. Trust me, the Universe can handle it!

Think of the process of using manure to help plants grow. Nobody thinks of excrement as a positive thing initially, but given the right circumstances, it becomes fertilizer, is very helpful to Mother Earth and actually helps us grow the fruits and vegetables we eat!

Letter writing can be very cathartic and actually allows

negative energy to be transmuted into something positive, much like the manure is used as fertilizer. Besides, negative emotions in the body are toxic and can turn into dis-ease.

The letter writing exercise can be used any time you feel the need to release some unexpressed emotions. It's possible you will need to write several letters (sometimes multiple letters to the same person) in order to feel at peace. Remember that these letters are for your eyes only; they aren't meant to be shared unless you decide to share them with a professional therapist.

Be sure to do something loving for yourself after your letter writing exercise. It could be that a cup of herbal tea and a nap are just the right thing, but trust yourself; you will know what feels best.

Step Five: Learn to say "No, thank you."

So often we are "programmed" to please others. We don't give our own feelings any voice and often dismiss our discomfort to please others. This results in feelings of resentment and an inability for us to love ourselves.

It is very empowering to learn to say "no." Toddlers have no trouble saying it and love to see the reactions from their parents when they do! No really is a powerful little word!

When I started learning to take better care of myself as an adult, I had to learn to say no because saying yes was literally making me sick. It was very interesting to watch the reactions of others and honestly, I quickly learned who my friends were.

Your friends will support your journey; they want the best for you. Others who have their own interests at heart will be disappointed and possibly resent you for not always being available to them. Please don't let other people put their guilt trips on you. If you are taking care of yourself, you are doing what's best for the planet; trust me!

Here are a couple of good tips for saying no in a productive way:

1) Let's say you are in the middle of something at home or work - it can be anything at all. The phone rings and it is one

of your friends.

This friend gossips about others and is always complaining about how awful her life is. When she doesn't have drama to complain about in her own life, she finds someone else to complain about. She rarely asks how you are because she is so wrapped up in herself.

You have started checking the caller ID to see if it's her because you want to avoid her, but every time y do that, you feel guilty. And the times you do answer the phone, she doesn't listen to you, even if you tell her you are on the way out and will have to call her back.

So, today, you answer the phone. You say hello, she says "hi" and immediately starts talking. You have just started to run a bath after a long day at work and you are exhausted. You don't have the energy to listen to her rants, so you very politely interrupt her (because she won't let you get a word in edgewise) and say "Excuse me. I'm sorry you are having a hard time right now, but I'm in the middle of something and I can't give you my undivided attention. I know that's not fair to you or to me, so let me call you back later when I can give you the attention you deserve. In the meantime, do something nice for yourself. Maybe you could call Sally or take a nice walk. Know that I care about you and I'll call you later."

She may ask what you are doing at the moment that's so important; don't tell her. You can say you don't have time to discuss it, or that it's none of her business; it's your choice.

The reality is, it's personal stuff that needs attention and you may choose to tell her, or not. She may get angry because you have always been available to her, but now you need to be available to YOU.

When someone asks you to do something you have always done but never wanted to, it's okay to say "No, thank you." It's a very interesting thing that the audacity of "no" diminishes greatly when "thank you" is added to it. For example:

No one ever thinks anything of it when the waiter comes back to the table after you've finished your dinner and asks if you'd like dessert. You say, "No, thank you." The waiter isn't insulted and neither is anyone else!

Let's try another example:

2) "Hi! I'm having a birthday party next Friday and of course I want you to be there. I even picked out some of the food I know you like."

Your response if you want to decline? "Oh, thanks so much for thinking of me; I'm sorry I won't be able to attend. Have a wonderful time, and I look forward to hearing all about it."

I guarantee you will start feeling better about yourself as you become comfortable with honoring how you are feeling inside instead of always thinking about what everyone else wants.

If you find yourself feeling guilty about saying no to others, remember that it isn't about being selfish; it's about loving yourself so you have love to give to others.

Keep practicing saying no. It will get easier, and creating healthy boundaries will become second nature to you.

Step Six: Affirmations

We live in such a fast paced world today, and there is no way to keep up with everything. We are bombarded with marketing messages that tell us we are: too fat or too thin, need more hair or less hair, need more money, more time, faster cars, more television stations, faster internet; it goes on and on. By the time we are adults, we have taken in hundreds of thousands of external messages!

These messages are designed to program us to be consumers and they have worked very well.

We also have our parent's words working in our subconscious at all times. These words can be negative or positive, but most of us have some subconscious negative thoughts influencing our current behavior.

In addition to the marketing and our parent's words, we have been influenced by friends, teachers, traumatic events, world events; many, many factors.

At the end of the day, these external messages have been internalized by us and the result is that we feel like we are not enough.

The truth is: we are all exactly where we are supposed to be at this moment. In this instant, we have an opportunity to change our lives or stay the same, lovingly accept who we are, or vow to be the person we were meant to be.

That person is inside you, possibly buried beneath a lot of years of pain and negative self-talk. You can change those negative, self-defeating thoughts!

Affirmations are an amazing way to re-program your thinking. I suggest two 20-30 minutes sessions each day dedicated to writing, saying and reading affirmations.

I suggest writing positive statements in the first, second and third person when doing this process. For example:

Let's say your sister was "the pretty one" in the family; you got the message loud and clear. Maybe you were "the smart one" or "the athletic one" but you wanted to be pretty and your family patronized you for it. Maybe they thought they were being supportive by telling you to stick to the things you were good it. In any case, you got the message, loud and clear, that you would never be loved for your beauty.

If this sounds harsh, trust me, I am only being candid. We internalize and exaggerate comments that make us feel "less than". Those messages become magnified in our subconscious and they influence decisions we make and how we feel about ourselves.

In order to change your subconscious thoughts about yourself, you have to bombard your conscious mind with the ideas you want to become your automatic way of thinking. So, going back to the example "I'm not pretty enough" ; in order to re-program that thinking, you'll write statements such as these:

I am pretty. She is pretty. Rebecca is pretty. You can also write your entire name; first, middle, last, followed by the statement.

I am beautiful. She is beautiful. (YOUR NAME HERE) is beautiful.

Here's an affirmation that I recommend to everyone. Please write it every time you do your affirmations:

I am loveable. She is loveable. (YOUR NAME HERE) is loveable.

Write the statements for at least five minutes each, until you have competed a 20 or 30 minute session. Then read aloud the statements you have written. Your voice can be very soft, barely audible if you like (depending on your surroundings), but saying the words aloud puts another depth of internalization to work for you and can expedite the re-programming process.

Of course, if you want to yell the affirmations (hopefully in a loving way) in the mirror, that's fine, too!

You'll find that the statements may evolve as you start writing; this is a good thing! It shows how connected our subconscious thoughts are to each other and how they work together to influence our perception of our self.

You may be wondering how long it will take to reprogram your brain. That's a good question, and the answer is that it varies from person to person. For most people, the process will take a few months. It could be one or two, or maybe as many as six.

I realize six months may sound daunting, but if the rest of your life can benefit from some time devoted to yourself each day or week, isn't it worth it? Besides, it took much longer than six months for your current thought patterns to be imprinted. It's amazing that you can change those thought patterns in a short amount of time with clear intention!

You can also expedite the process by recording tapes of your affirmations and listening to them right before you go to sleep. I always suggest you record them yourself, rather than have someone else's voice on the recording.

In a few weeks, you'll most likely start feeling a bit more grounded and centered - more connected to your own thoughts. You may also start to feel a deeper sense of peace and calm, sure signs that you are starting to feel love for yourself.

You are loveable!

Epilogue

What is a perfect life?   Only you can define it for YOU;   it's the life YOU want to be living!

In it, you wake up happy, energized, excited to see what the day will bring!   You are fully present with yourself, your family and loved ones, experiencing each moment with full attention and intention.

Remember, we are all works in progress and we will be until the end of our days.

I wish you joy, peace and love in every moment of your life.

In gratitude,
Rebecca

About the Author

Rebecca is a psychic who has been using her intuition to help people for over twenty years. Her journey into the world of psychic phenomenon started when she was 21 and began working as a police dispatcher. It was then that she noticed strong reactions in her "gut" to people or situations that were unusual.

Rebecca didn't think too much about those odd occurrences; she just thought her "sixth sense" was becoming more keen since she worked in law enforcement. A few years later, she went with a friend to see a psychic who told her she had very strong guidance and needed to pay attention to it. At that time, Rebecca had embarked on a spiritual journey by reading books, learning about meditation, the effects of prayer, and developing a deeper awareness of energy and how it affects us.

Today, Rebecca has many happy clients around the world. She "sees", "hears" and "feels" information, instead of using tarot cards or other tools to assist her in her work.

Visit Rebecca at: www.iamrebecca.com